Start Writing Adventure Stories

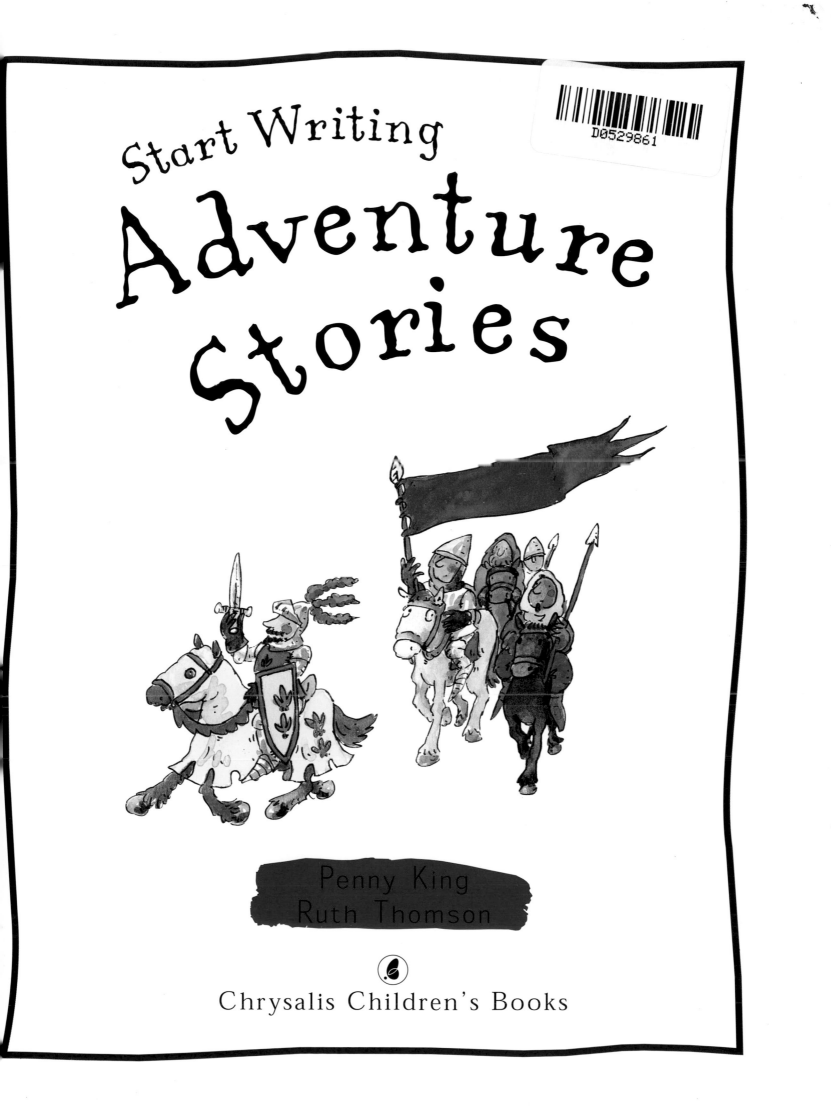

Penny King
Ruth Thomson

Chrysalis Children's Books

First published in the UK in 2000 by
Chrysalis Children's Books
An imprint of Chrysalis Books Group Plc
The Chrysalis Building
Bramley Road
London W10 6SP

Paperback edition first published in 2001

ISBN 1 84138 207 8 (hardback)
ISBN 1 84138 214 0 (paperback)

British Library in Publication Data for this book
is available from the British Library.

hb: 10 9 8 7 6 5 4 3 2
pb: 10 9 8 7 6 5 4

Series editors: Mary-Jane Wilkins,
Stephanie Turnbull
Designers: Rachel Hamdi, Angie Allison,
Holly Mann
Illustrators: Brenda Haw, Jan McCafferty,
Gwyneth Williamson
Educational consultants: Pie Corbett, Poet and
Consultant to the National Literacy Strategy;
Sarah Mullen, Literacy Consultant

Printed in China

Contents

WRITING STORIES

Have you ever wondered
how to start a story
or what to write next?
This book will help you.

★

There are six big pictures like this.
Each picture gives you lots of ideas
for a story. All the words on the
picture are <u>nouns</u> (names of things)
and you can use them to check
your spelling.

Each big picture is followed by
a story plan. The plan is divided
into parts to help you write exciting
stories with a beginning, a middle
and an end. The story plan also
helps you to decide what kind of
story to write.

★

The story begins

First think about where the story
takes place and decide what might
have happened so far. You need
an exciting opening sentence.

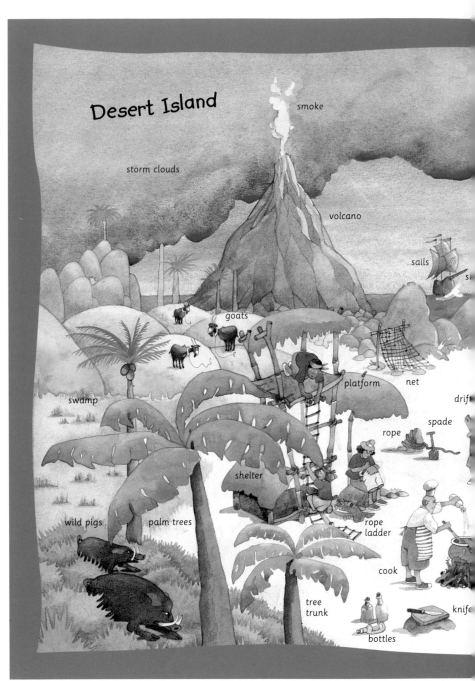

Desert Island

smoke

storm clouds

volcano

sails

goats

platform

net

drif

swamp

spade

rope

shelter

rope
ladder

wild pigs

palm trees

cook

tree
trunk

knife

bottles

The characters

Next, think about the characters.
How do your main characters feel?
Use <u>adjectives</u> (describing words)
to help you. The more interesting
you make the characters, the
more exciting your story will be.

Is this character
a hero, heroine
or a villain?

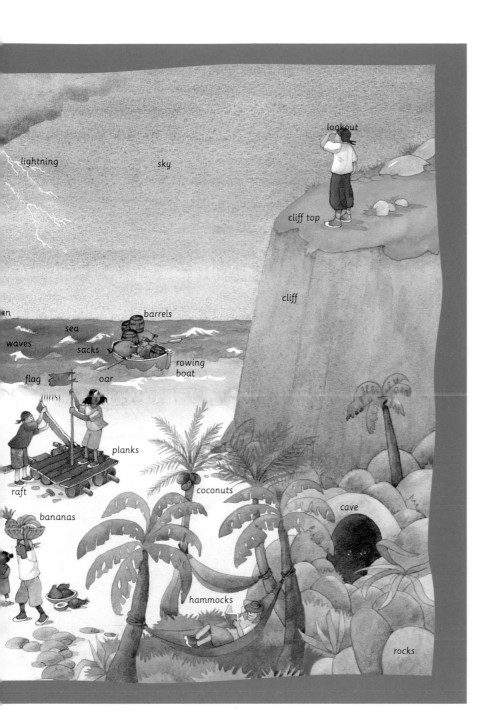

lightning

sky

lookout

cliff top

cliff

barrels

sea

waves

sacks

rowing boat

flag

oar

planks

raft

coconuts

cave

bananas

hammocks

rocks

The problem

Adventure stories are action packed! You are the writer and anything can happen.

Perhaps you are attacked...

or disaster strikes...

or something completely unexpected happens.

The resolution

Finally, decide how to end the adventure. What happens? Readers like to know what happens to all the characters. You can choose a happy, sad or surprising ending.

The setting

Each story is set in a different place. Use your senses to help you describe each place. Think about what you might see, hear, smell, touch and taste.

grassy
leafy

rocky
stony

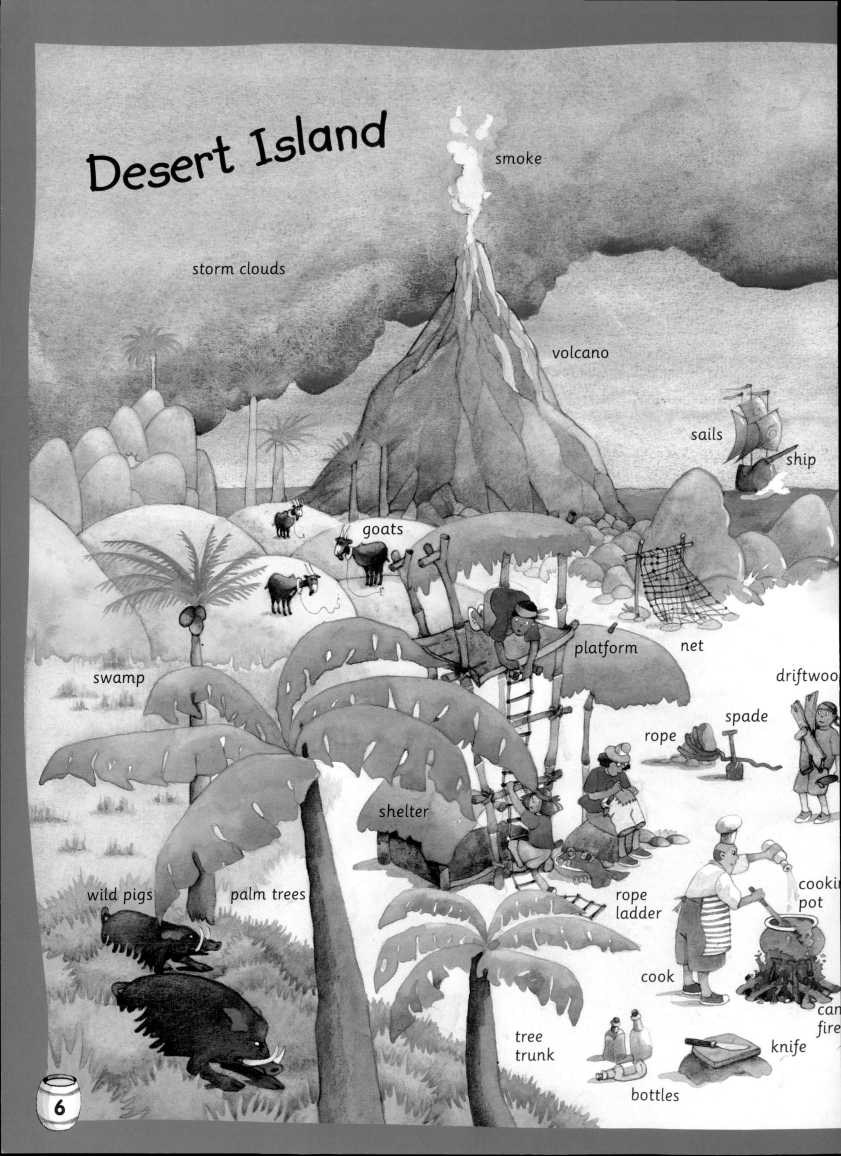

Desert Island

smoke

storm clouds

volcano

sails

ship

goats

platform

net

swamp

driftwoo

spade

rope

shelter

wild pigs

palm trees

rope
ladder

cooki
pot

cook

tree
trunk

can
fire

knife

bottles

6

lookout

sky

lightning

cliff top

cliff

rlzon

barrels

sea

waves

sacks

rowing
boat

flag

oar

mast

shore

planks

raft

coconuts

cave

eapple

bananas

basket

hammocks

rocks

d

7

THE STORY BEGINS

You are on a desert island.
There are many dangers.
You are the hero or heroine.
You have to decide how
to save everyone's life.

Why are you there?
★ Is it your home?
★ Are you shipwrecked?
★ Are you looking for something?

THE CHARACTERS

★ Who lives with you on the island?

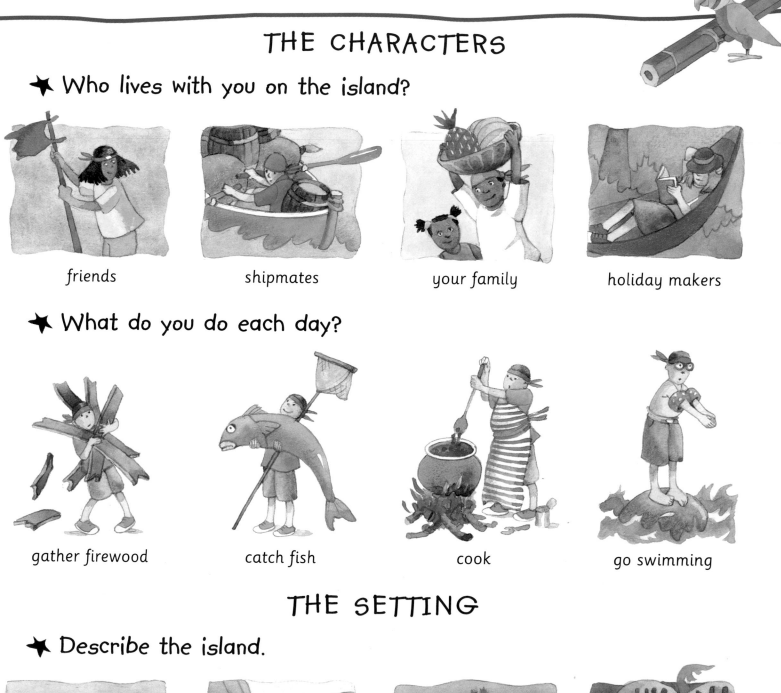

friends

shipmates

your family

holiday makers

★ What do you do each day?

gather firewood

catch fish

cook

go swimming

THE SETTING

★ Describe the island.

dry
sandy

rocky
stony

marshy
swampy

grassy
leafy

THE PROBLEM

★ Danger ahead! What is it?

creak
splash

A strange ship is approaching.

roar
bellow
snort
rustle

A wild beast attacks.

boom
whoosh
rumble

The volcano erupts.

flash
crash

A storm breaks.

Use phrases like these:
To my horror...
I looked up and suddenly saw...
All at once there was a loud...
Out of the blue...

How do you feel?
What do you see?
What do you hear?

THE RESOLUTION

★ What happens
   in the end?

Do you:
   ★ hide, and if so, where?
   ★ lead everyone to safety?
   ★ sail away on your raft?
   ★ fight the strangers?

gates

park

path

puter

banner

band

flag

antennae

leader

platform

chauffeur

president

bodyguard

ramp

steps

im

robot

video
camera

megaphone

limousine

11

THE STORY BEGINS

A UFO has landed in the city centre. Crowds gather in the park to see this astonishing sight. The president hopes the aliens are friendly and has arranged a splendid welcome party.

Decide why the aliens have landed.

★ Has their planet been destroyed?
★ Do they want to conquer earth?
★ Is there something on earth that they desperately need?

THE CHARACTERS

★ Describe the people in your story.

The president could be:

powerful
worried
welcoming
anxious
friendly

The children could be:

inventive
brave
foolish
curious
fearless

The alien leader could be:

threate
hope
cunn
menac
grate

How does he communicate?

THE SETTING

★ Describe the UFO.

enormous
colossal

glistening
gleaming

puzzling
mysterious

shiny
metallic

eerie
strange

smoking
steaming

glowing
flashing

THE PROBLEM

★ Suddenly the unexpected happens.

Do the aliens attack?

★ What sounds can you hear?

click 'hiss' roar
oompah oompah
chuggah chuggah murmur
nee-naw nee-naw

Does the UFO take off,
leaving the leader behind?

Are the children
kidnapped by the aliens?

Does the President transform
himself into an alien?

Does the alien leader grab
the thing he needs? What is it?

THE RESOLUTION

★ How does the story end?

Remember to tell
your readers what
happens to all
the characters.

★ Do the two leaders make
a deal?

★ Is there a battle?

★ What do the children do?

★ Do the aliens leave or stay?

Princess in Peril

castle

princess

battlements

window

keep

pi

steps

meadow

king

horses

queen

wood

guard

cauldron

spit

fire

anvil

blacksmith

soldier

wall

sheep

moat

14

THE STORY BEGINS

A princess is locked in a
tower guarded by two soldiers.
Has she been kidnapped?
Has she done something
terrible and been imprisoned?
Or is she waiting to be rescued?

Here are some ways to begin.

★ No one will find me in the tower...

★ 'She'll never escape,' chuckled
the king.

★ 'How dare they attack me!'
thundered the princess.

THE CHARACTERS

★ Think about the main characters.

Is the princess kind and beautiful?
She could be:

vain
spoilt

superhuman
bloodthirsty

Is the prince brave and handsome?
He could be:

big-headed
greedy

cowardly
clumsy

THE SETTING

★ Where is the castle?

on a hill

beyond the forest

near a village

Is the castle well-kept or is it shabby and dirty?

THE PROBLEM

★ Explain what happens to the princess.

Does she manage to escape? How?

Does she want to be rescued?

Does someone save her life?

Do kidnappers exchange her for riches, power or land?

★ Add excitement to your story with phrases such as:

Without warning...
Bursting through the door...

Out of the darkness leapt...
In a flash...

THE RESOLUTION

★ What happens in the end?

Write an unexpected ending to surprise your readers.

★ Who triumphs?
★ What do they gain?
★ Do the princess and the prince live happily ever after?

Neptune's Kingdom

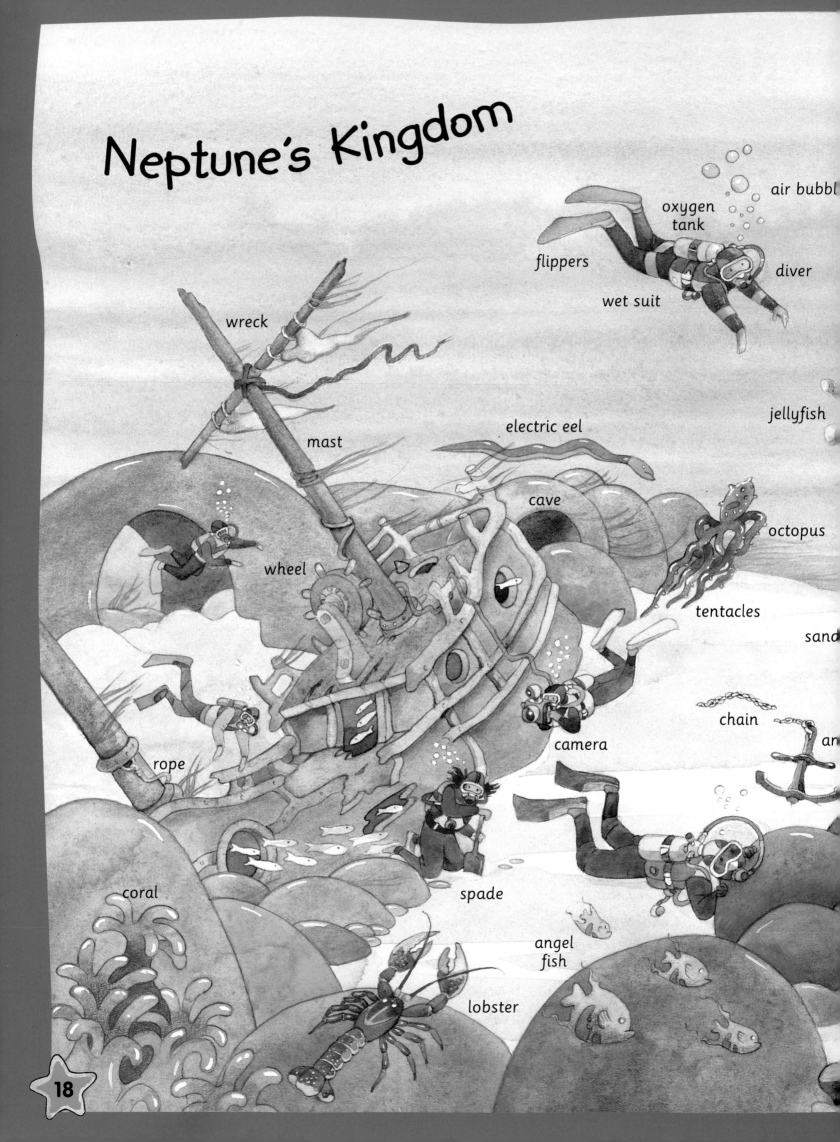

air bubbl

oxygen tank

flippers

wet suit

diver

wreck

jellyfish

mast

electric eel

cave

octopus

wheel

tentacles

sand

rope

chain

an

camera

coral

spade

angel fish

lobster

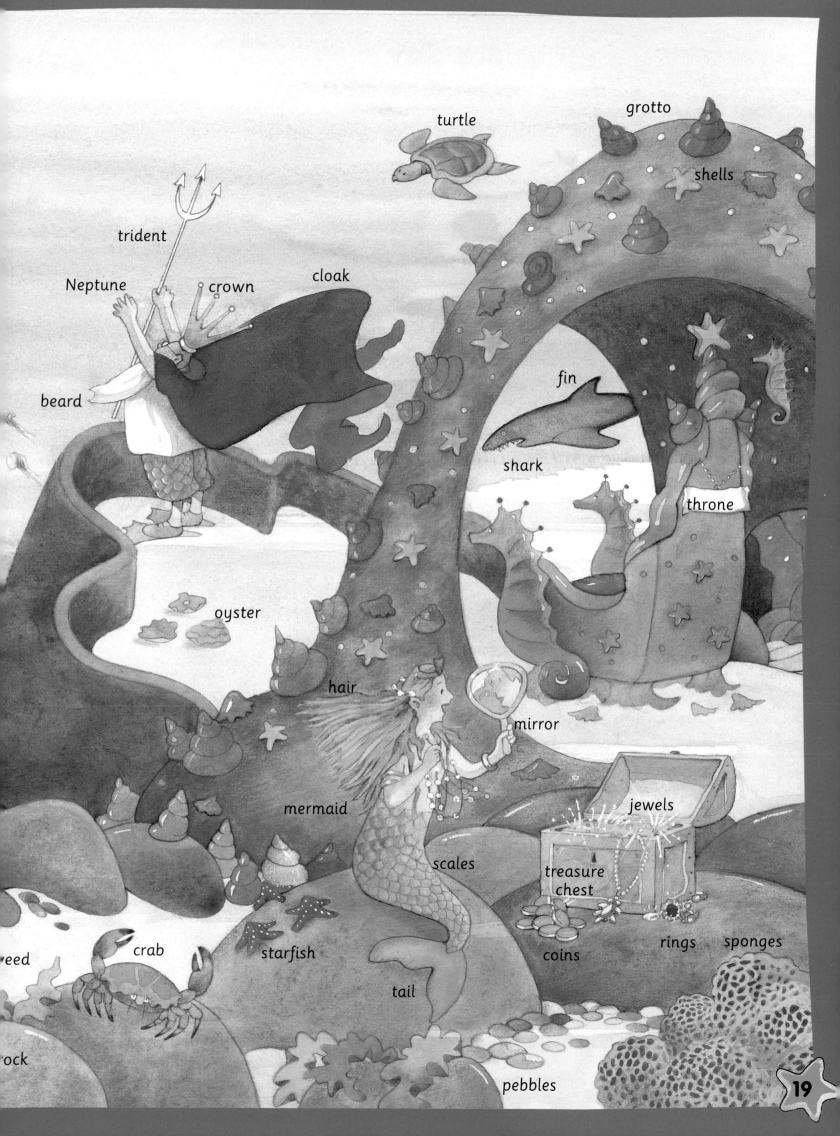

turtle

grotto

shells

trident

Neptune

crown

cloak

beard

fin

shark

throne

oyster

hair

mirror

mermaid

jewels

scales

treasure chest

eed

crab

starfish

coins

rings

sponges

tail

ock

pebbles

19

THE STORY BEGINS

Divers have discovered
Neptune's kingdom.
Neptune is an old man,
but he has magic powers.
His kingdom is full
of priceless treasure.

Why have the divers come?
- ★ Are they looking for something?
- ★ Has Neptune asked them
  to come?
- ★ Are they lost?

THE CHARACTERS

★ Decide who to be – a diver, a mermaid or Neptune.

The divers could be:

daring	greedy
curious	adventurous
terrified	bewitched

The mermaid could be:

grateful	annoyed
glad	startled
fearful	excited

Neptune could be:

angry	worried
alarmed	horrified
surprised	amazed

THE SETTING

★ Describe the things you can see.

soggy
spongy

smooth
round

shiny
sparkling

wriggling
gliding

THE PROBLEM

★ **What happens when Neptune and the mermaid meet the divers?**

Does Neptune:

- assemble a fishy army?
- trick the divers?
- help them?

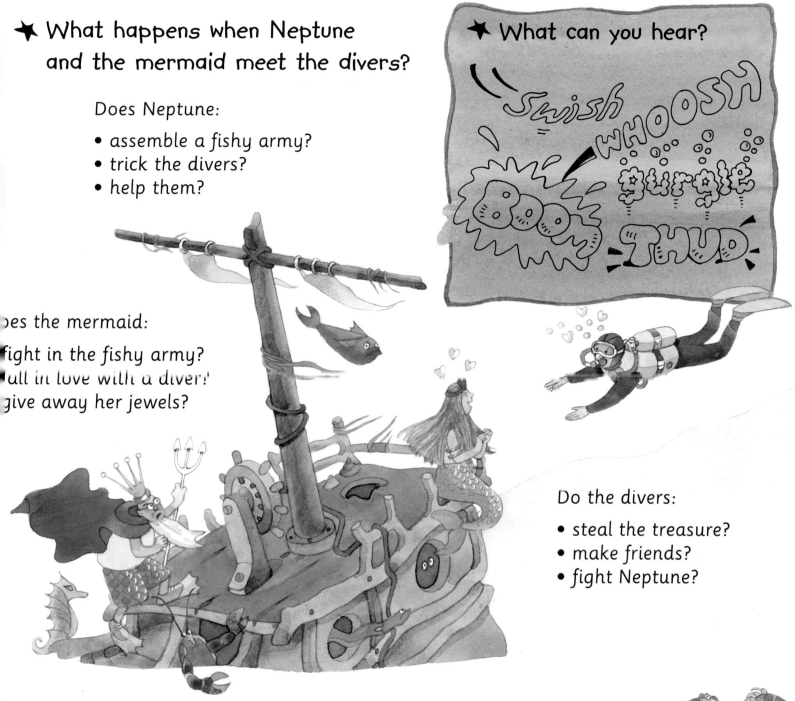

★ **What can you hear?**

Swish WHOOSH gurgle BOOM THUD

Does the mermaid:

- fight in the fishy army?
- fall in love with a diver?
- give away her jewels?

Do the divers:

- steal the treasure?
- make friends?
- fight Neptune?

THE RESOLUTION

★ **How does your story end?**

Here are some ideas for the last line. How could you lead up to this ending?

★ Neptune never saw the divers again.

★ The divers never told anyone about Neptune's Kingdom.

★ The mermaid missed her jewels, but she was proud of saving Neptune.

Rainforest Race

leaves

canopy

onkey

boa
constrictor

lars

tent

hammock

fern

map

backpack

compass

visor

alligator

tracks

sketch
book

flask

paddle

boulder

boots

torch

sleeping
bag

fishing rod

canoe

ants

23

THE STORY BEGINS

Hidden in the middle of a hot, sticky rainforest is something very precious. You set off to look for it, but discover that other people are looking for it too.

What are you looking for?
- ★ A rare flower that cures diseases?
- ★ A lost city?
- ★ A missing person?
- ★ Treasure?

THE CHARACTERS

★ Decide which character to be.

Choose words to describe yourself and the other characters.

determined
unselfish
ruthless
greedy
tough
thoughtless
adventurous

THE SETTING

★ What is the rainforest like?

shady
shadowy

hot
damp

steamy
misty

brilliant
colourful

THE PROBLEM

★ On your search you might come across...

a broken bridge

a raging torrent

★ What can you hear?

chattering
rustling
howling
hissing
squawking
screeching

a swarm of insects

ferocious animals

★ These could be clues that you are nearly there.

footprints

smoke from a fire

a funny smell

a sign on a tree

★ Remember your rivals. Can you stop them getting there first?

THE RESOLUTION

★ What happens in the end?
Did you find what
you were looking for
or have the others
beaten you to it?

★ Do you become famous?
★ Will you share your discovery?
★ Can you do a deal?
★ Are you overjoyed
or disappointed?

The Marvellous Machine

spanners hammer drill saw mallet pliers file

clock

lamp

torch

screws nails

screwdrivers

paints
paintbrushes

vice

plans

oil can

robot

cloth

toolbox

spring

steps

mop

bucket

tins

trolley

THE STORY BEGINS

A magnificent machine is hidden in a secret factory. It is the only one in the world. A spy has crept in to find out all about it.

What is special about the machine?
- ★ What does it make?
- ★ How does it work?
- ★ Why is it so secret?

THE CHARACTERS

★ Describe the characters.

One of them could be the spy! Are they:

happy and cheerful
or
cunning and sly

hard-working and clever
or
wicked and scheming

helpful and friendly
or
secretive and sneaky

hot and tired
or
nervous and worried

THE SETTING

★ What is the machine room like?

steamy
smoky

noisy
deafening

messy
untidy

tidy
organized

THE PROBLEM

★ **What goes wrong?**

Has someone spotted the spy?

Has the machine been reprogrammed?

Does the machine behave oddly?

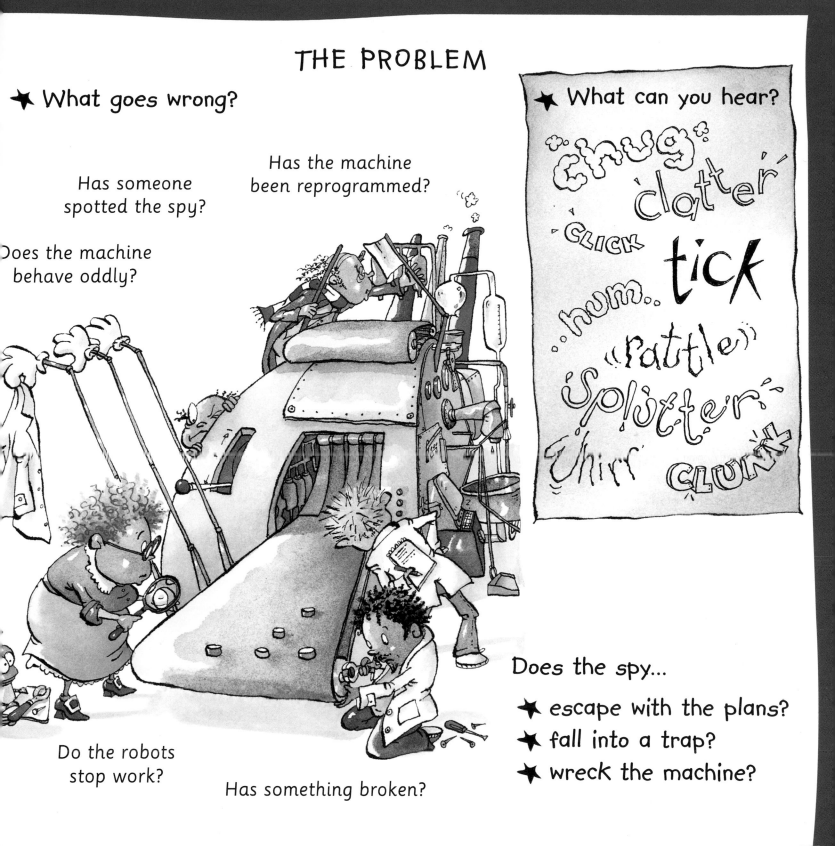

★ **What can you hear?**

chug clatter CLICK hum tick rattle splutter whirr CLUNK

Do the robots stop work?

Has something broken?

Does the spy...

★ escape with the plans?
★ fall into a trap?
★ wreck the machine?

THE RESOLUTION

★ What happens in the end? Your story can end with success for the spy or for the workers.

★ What becomes of the machine?
★ Does the factory stay a secret?
★ What happens to all the characters?

WRITING TIPS

Here are some useful tips
to help you start writing
brilliant adventure stories.

What do I need?

First you need to find
a quiet place to write.
You can write with
a pencil on paper or
straight on to a computer. Once you
have written your story you
may want to add some
illustrations.

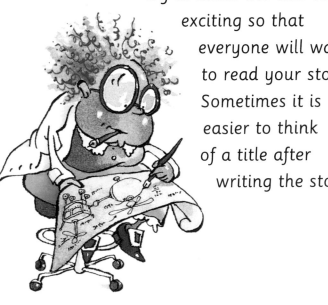

How do I choose a title?

You could use the story headings in this
book, or you could invent your own title.
Try to make the title sound
exciting so that
everyone will want
to read your story.
Sometimes it is
easier to think
of a title after
writing the story.

How do I start my story?

If you write a gripping opening
everyone will want to read the story.
Here are some ideas.

• Start with one word and
an exclamation mark –
Stop! Run! Help! NO! Quick! Crash!

• Start with a question –
'Where are you going?' asked Sally.

• Start with the name of your main
character – Jim stared out to sea.

How do I make my characters sound real?

Invent two or three main characters and decide what they are like. Use adjectives to describe them. What sort of people are they – nervous or brave, serious or funny? Are they heroes or villains? How do they speak and what do they say? Make sure they stay the same all through the story!

How do I work out what happens?

Decide how the problem is solved – does the hero or heroine save the day, or does the villain win? Work out what the ending will be before starting to write, and don't forget to say what happens to all the characters. Finish with a really good last line. See if you can think of something more exciting than 'They all lived happily ever after.'

What should I write about?

You need to think of a problem for your characters to face. Maybe they are in danger. What if a wild animal escaped from a zoo? What if someone cast a wicked spell? You can use the ideas in this book or create your own. Remember to use lots of description.